Herobrine Scared Stiff

Book 2

Zack Zombie Books

Chapter 1
One Strange Ritual

Trick-or-treating is so weird! It seems like on Halloween any kid on the planet can walk up to any house and get free candy. But, it only works if they're dressed up. I know that coming from The Minecraft Overworld is weird, and having a square-shaped body is really weird, but the more I learn about Halloween, the weirder my life gets!

The whole thing is really quite bizarre, but as the school bell rang for the end of the day, I decided it was something I wanted check out a little more.

All the kids at Butts Road Middle School flooded out of the main entrance as quickly as they could. It was a Thursday afternoon, but instead of heading home to play computer games and watch TV, it appeared there was something else going on.

"Come on, Herobrine," my friend Lucy Lurker shouted as she ran ahead of me, down the school steps and made her way to the gate. "It's Halloween and we're having a party at my house tonight. Loads of our friends will be coming. If you want to go trick-or-treating first, we'll have to get a move on."

I followed Lucy as quickly as I could. Lucy was really excited and moving at quite a speed. This was actually quicker than I'd normally walk. But I hobbled along with my rectangular legs as fast as I could. I was desperate to find out more about this thing the human world calls Halloween.

"So, what else happens on Halloween besides getting free candy from people's houses?" I asked.

"Loads! Halloween is one of the coolest nights of the year. You see all kinds of things like ghosts, goblins, and wizards."

Weird. I thought. *I didn't know they had those in the human world.*

"I'm going to be a witch tonight. Mom picked up my outfit this afternoon. I can't wait to see it."

Lucy's a witch? Whoa, she never told me that!

At first, as we headed through town everything seemed like a normal evening to me, but then I began to notice a few differences. I spotted the silhouettes of black cats in a few windows and the occasional broomstick leaning against a store wall. This was pretty weird, but I figured that someone probably just left them there after cleaning up after the cats.

Then, we turned into Lucy's street and I hardly recognized it. It was the strangest looking street I had ever seen.

Large, inflatable orange pumpkins hung from every tree. I looked closer. The pumpkins had funny looking faces printed on them.

The same pumpkins sat on people's brick walls and at the end of their drives, but those pumpkins looked real and the faces were carved into them. I suddenly began to get a feeling of what Halloween was all about.

"Is this Halloween thing some sort of Pumpkin Festival?" I asked

Lucy laughed. "Not quite! We just carve faces into them and put them in front of our houses for decoration."

"Oh! Like an offering to the Nether Gods?"

"No. They're not there to be eaten, silly. We carve them out and put candles inside them to light them up. We'll be making some at my house in a bit."

"We have pumpkins where I come from," I said, "Except we don't carve them, we just put them on our heads."

"Oh, OK. If you say so," Lucy said with a really confused look on her face.

I really thought I could figure out what was going on. But now I realized that I didn't have a clue!

And, no matter how Lucy explained it, I thought Halloween was the strangest thing I had ever seen. Roaming ghosts, goblins, and wizards, mixed with carving out pumpkins and collecting candy from people's houses was definitely a weird combination. But since I was living in the human world now, I realized that I might as well figure out what this Halloween craziness was all about.

Chapter 2
Party at Lucy's House

We got to Lucy's house and headed up the handful of stone steps that led to her front door. Her place was practically the only house in the street that wasn't covered in weird decorations. But, Lucy assured me all that was about to change.

"Hi, mom!" Lucy shouted as we burst through the door. "Did you pick up my outfit and the pumpkins?"

"Certainly did, dear," Mrs. Lurker replied. "Everything is ready. Your outfit is on your bed and the pumpkins are over there on the kitchen table. But, before you get started, make sure you sit down and have a quick snack. You kids have got a long night ahead."

Lucy's mom had prepared us orange juice and a few sandwiches. She was making loads for the party later, but had put some aside to keep us going. Lucy ate hers quicker than I'd ever seen anyone eat anything before. Then, she ran to the kitchen drawer, found the pumpkin carving tools and sat down at the kitchen table. I'd never carved any pumpkins before, so I was actually quite excited.

There was a fruit bowl in the middle of the table and, as this was my first time, I decided to start with something a little smaller until I got the hang of it. I picked up a banana and began to carve a smiley mouth into it. I have to admit, my carved banana ended up looking pretty good. But, as soon as Lucy saw it she grabbed it from me and dropped it into the trash.

"Carve this," she said, pushing the smaller of the two pumpkins in front of me. "Just watch what I do."

Lucy cut a circle in the top of the pumpkin, pulled it off and then started scooping out the insides. The inside of a pumpkin was wet and slimy. But, the seeds were a lot of fun. I found that if I laid a line of them on the table and then slammed my square arm onto them, they'd shoot off across the room and hit the kitchen window. I could have done it all night, but Lucy's mom didn't really appreciate my new game. Plus, Mrs. Lurker was beginning to get quite annoyed because I was firing them faster than she could sweep them up.

Once the pumpkins were hollowed out, I watched as Lucy began to design a face on the front of hers. She used a pen to draw it and then started cutting it out.

I picked up the pen and decided to create a design for mine as well. I've always had a square head, so I always wanted to see what I'd look like if my head was... well, round. So I carved two rectangular eyes in the top half of the pumpkin and then used some brown paint to create the hair on top and the mouth area at the bottom. It only took a few minutes and when I was done. I was pretty impressed.

"There, what do you think?" I asked, spinning the pumpkin round to show Lucy.

"Uh... a bit weird," Lucy replied. "You haven't done much carving. You've just carved two rectangular slots. I don't even know what it's supposed to be. It should have looked some-thing like this."

Lucy turned her pumpkin around. She'd carved a face with scary, triangular-eyes, a triangular nose and a jagged mouth with sharp teeth.

"Your pumpkin looks constipated," I said.

I don't think Lucy appreciated my comment because after I said it, she took her knife and stabbed it into my pumpkin.

Mrs. Lurker switched off the kitchen lights and lit two small candles. She carried them carefully to the kitchen table and put inside the pumpkins.

"Oh!" Lucy looked at the glowing eyes on my pumpkin and then at me. Then she realized the pumpkin was supposed to look like me. But, even after she got it, she didn't seem impressed. I think she was still mad about her constipated pumpkin.

Mrs. Lurker took the pumpkins outside and put them on the wall near the front door. Meanwhile, Lucy went up to get dressed. I'd never seen a witch up close before, even though there are plenty of witches where I come from. So I headed upstairs as well to see what a spooky witch from the human world looked like.

"Wow! Look at this!" Lucy shouted, picking up the outfit that lay on her bed. "It's perfect!"

The witch's outfit was black and had a long pointy hat. It also came with a broomstick and a beaky-looking extra nose.

"Wow. I didn't know you carried your nose around in a plastic bag," I said.

Lucy gave me another one of her confused looks.

"It sure is small compared to the noses on the witches that I'm used to."

"It's just a typical type of witch's nose," Lucy said as she pulled it from the plastic bag. "Here, why don't you try it on?"

I thought it was kind of gross that Lucy shared her nose with me. But I took the nose and she pulled the elastic thread around the back of my big square head and positioned the snarled up nose on the front of my flat face. Lucy laughed as I wandered into the bathroom to check myself out in the mirror.

I'd never had a nose that protruded from my face, so when I saw it in the mirror it was kind of a shock. It was the weirdest thing I'd ever seen. I wanted to take a closer look up my new nose to see what I would find, so I leaned towards the mirror. But, as I did I slipped and accidentally pushed the nose into the electric socket by the mirror. There was a spark and a little fire. Next thing I know the entire nose started melting and it fell onto the floor in a matter of seconds. I didn't know what to do. Lucy's nose was gone and the room smelled like burnt plastic.

I opened the window to get rid of the smell and used a towel to help waft it out. Then, Lucy came in.

"Thanks for lighting a match," she said, making a funny face. "Hey, where's my witches nose?"

I looked at the melted nose on the floor and dropped the towel over it to cover up the evidence. Then, I looked at the window.

"A bird stole it," I hastily replied.

"A bird stole my nose?" Lucy questioned.

"Yep! Swooped in, took the nose and flew away."

Lucy gave me a look that made me think she didn't believe me. But she just shook her head and didn't say anything more about it.

Wow, I guess people aren't that attached to their noses in the human world, I thought.

I followed Lucy back into her bedroom, closing the bathroom door firmly behind me, and watched as she put on the witches hat and picked up her broomstick. With her witches outfit complete, she looked me up and down and scratched her hairy chin.

"We never got a costume for you, did we?"

I shook my head. Lucy looked around her bedroom. Her eyes lit up.

"I know what we can do," she whispered. "But don't tell my mom!"

We sneaked into the spare bedroom, and she pulled the large white sheet off the bed and threw it on the floor. Then, she crept downstairs and returned with a pair of scissors. She closed the door to the spare room and then cut two rectangular holes in the middle of the sheet.

"There! Perfect," she said, putting the scissors on the dressing table and holding up the sheet beside me.

"What is?"

"This will be your costume," she exclaimed.

"Oh! Am I going as a bed?"

"No. You're going to be a Halloween Herobrine Ghost! Perfect for haunting."

"Thanks. I've never been...Err...a ghost before."

Wow, in my world you usually had to die to become a ghost. Here you only need a bedsheet. So strange...

"No problem, Herobrine," Lucy replied, throwing the sheet over my head and then pulling it into position. "You look awesome."

After my ghostly transformation, we headed back downstairs. Lucy wanted to keep me hidden though. She said that if her mom found out that she had taken a sheet from the spare bed and cut holes in it, she'd get grounded. Didn't really know what that meant, so I just stayed at the bottom stair as Lucy dashed into the kitchen. She grabbed two buckets for trick-or-treating and sneaked out through the front door. I hobbled after her, really excited to see what would happen.

Lucy closed the door quietly behind us and we descended the steps into the street, and it looked like the whole human world had gone crazy!

Chapter 3
The Minecraft Portal

The entire street was filled with the weirdest and spookiest creatures I had ever seen. I took a step back in fear for our safety.

"Don't worry. They're harmless," Lucy reassured me. She was so confident; it was like she had a heart of steel.

Lucy giggled and wandered off into the street to find a house to go trick-or-treating. Clouds had formed overhead and there was an eerie feeling in the air. I decided I wanted to keep close to Lucy on this particular night, so I stayed by her side.

As we moved down the street my vision was slightly blocked as the sheet kept slipping over my eyes. I had to keep adjusting it so I could see where I was going.

Man, being a ghost is a lot of work, I thought.

The first door we knocked on belonged to one of Lucy's neighbors, Mr. Gesundheit.

Lucy knocked on his door three times. Inside we could hear a lot of noise and loads of sneezing. Mr. Gesundheit eventually answered.

"Sorry it took me a while," the red-nosed man said, holding a handkerchief to his face. "You caught me in the middle of a bit of a...Ah...ah...ah...ah..."

Lucy held out her trick-or-treating bucket and Mr. Gesundheit looked like he was preparing to sneeze into it. But it died down, as soon as Lucy pulled it back. Next thing you know Mr. Gesundheit looked at me and said... "HACHOO!"

"I know it's Halloween and all, but I didn't know getting slimed was part of the deal," I said as I wiped the green slime off my ghostly face.

Lucy didn't know what to say, so she just held out her bucket, and so I did it too. Mr. Gesundheit disappeared into the house for moment and then reappeared with a tub of candy. He dropped a piece of candy into each of our buckets. As he was about to go back into his house, he let out the biggest sneeze yet, right into his tub of candy.

"I guess the next group of kids who get candy are in for a real surprise," Lucy said with a laugh. But then we looked at each other as we sucked on the candy we just got.

As we walked further down the street, Lucy suddenly spotted a friend she knew who was dressed like a princess. She left me standing there and went running ahead of me. I decided to walk slowly to catch up so that my sheet wouldn't fall off. As I was hobbling toward Lucy, I noticed more of the weirdly decorated houses. They all looked really creepy. Then, one particular house caught my attention. It looked creepier than the rest and, as I peered over the garden fence, I saw something in the back garden that seemed kind of weirdly familiar. I sneaked through the side gate and hid behind a bush to see what was going on.

In the garden, several kids were standing around. One seemed to be in charge. He was a wizard boy and he wore a long, pointed blue hat with golden stars on it and a long blue velvet gown. There was something in his hand...a white wooden staff. But, as I looked further into the garden, it was the object in front of him that terrified me to my very core. Standing in the middle of the garden at twice the height of the boy was a gigantic Minecraft Portal. It had a huge black obsidian frame and a glowing purple area in the center - there was no mistaking it!

I crouched lower and watched as the wizard boy spoke.

"It's Halloween night and we're about to summon the Zombies and Creepers from the Minecraft world and bring them into the real world."

What! I thought, as I ducked lower so that they wouldn't see me. *They're not crazy enough to bring Zombies and Creepers into this world, are they?*

The wizard boy lifted his staff in the air as a chilling wind blew through the garden. The group of other kids cheered him on.

"I shall now hold up my magic staff and chant three times," the wizard boy said. "And when the magic is complete, the Minecraft mobs will travel through the portal. Be prepared for anything!"

I could hardly move. I was terrified. It felt like my body had turned to stone and rooted me to the spot.

"Minecraft mobs appear, Minecraft mobs appear, Minecraft mobs appear!"

I fixed my stare on the purple haze in the center of the portal and hoped with everything I had that his chants didn't work. But then, the purple haze parted and a Minecraft Zombie leapt though! I fell backwards into a bush with shock. But it seemed that the Zombie wasn't the only one. Another followed, then out from the portal came two Creepers. Then the purple haze closed.

I couldn't believe it. Minecraft Zombies and Creepers have invaded the human world!

Chapter 4
Preparing for the Party

I wanted to run out and warn everybody, but I was too scared to move. What if there were more mobs coming out? Or what if they pushed me into the portal?!! I couldn't take the risk. I held tight and continued to watch.

The more I watched, the weirder things got. The wizard boy and the other kids joked around like it was normal to have man-eating Zombies and exploding Creepers hanging around. Suddenly, the wizard boy's mom called to the kids from the kitchen doorway. The kids ran into the house and, to my complete surprise, the Zombies and Creepers ran in too. This was serious. I had to warn people or human life as they knew it would be totally over.

I crept out from behind the bush and tiptoed down the side path and through the garden gate into the street. As I backed away, I bumped into someone. I was so scared I screamed like a little girl! What was behind me? Could it be another Creeper? As I turned around, I breathed a huge sigh of relief. Luckily, it was only Lucy lurking behind me.

"Where have you been?" she asked. "I've been searching all over for you. We need to get home. My friends are coming over soon for the Halloween party."

"But I just saw Zombies and Creepers!"

"We haven't got any more time for that now. We've still got lots to prepare at home. Come on!"

Wow. Lucy must have a heart of steel.

After what I told her, she just acted like having man-eating Zombies and exploding Creepers in her neighborhood were no big deal.

I looked back at the spooky house and could just about see in through the living room window. The kids now seemed be playing a game, but I couldn't see the Minecraft mobs anywhere. I squinted harder because the room was so dark. Suddenly, a Creeper sprung up at the window and stared straight at me. I panicked and ran for my life. I caught up with Lucy, jumped up the steps to her house and slammed the door behind me.

"What's all the noise for?" Mrs. Lurker asked, not looking up from the sandwiches she was preparing in the kitchen. "It sounds like a herd of elephants came storming through the door."

Noticing that I was still wearing the bedsheet from the spare bed, Lucy quickly pulled it off of me and threw it into the cupboard under the stairs.

"Sorry for making such a noise, Mrs. Lurker," I replied. "I'm just... err... excited to be at my first Halloween party."

"Good for you, Herobrine," she replied. "Now both of you come here and help me carry this food over to the dinning room table."

The food Mrs. Lurker had prepared looked amazing. There were mini finger sausages, potato chips, fruit and all kinds of sandwiches. They even had my favorite human food, cheese squares!

"Do we need to carve this fruit too?" I asked, heading to the kitchen drawer to get the carving tools.

Lucy and her mom gave me a strange look and then continued putting the food out. Once everything was ready, we took out some orange and black decorations and hung them up around the room. I was given the task of helping Lucy pin things up. I guess my square head made a good step stool.

Once the decorating was done. It was time to prepare some Halloween party games. Mrs.

Lurker had everything organized, so Lucy and I did our best to help.

The first thing we did was take a tray of donuts into the garden. Lucy had to tie some string around each donut and then my job was to hang the donuts from a pole just above my head.

"What's this for?" I asked.

"We do this every year. This is a game called the Donut Eating Race. We each have to wear a blindfold and then try to be the quickest to eat a donut."

"Oh! Wouldn't it be quicker if you just served it on a plate?" I asked.

"Of course, but it wouldn't be as much fun. Now head inside and get the next things from mom."

I went back inside to see Mrs. Lurker. To my surprise, she was holding several rolls of toilet paper and dumped them into my arms.

"I don't think I have to go right now, Mrs. Lurker," I said.

"No, no...they're for the party. They need to stay down here," Mrs. Lurker said. "Put them on the couch will you, Herobrine?"

I did as she asked, but I was confused as to why the toilet paper was being put on the couch.

Lucy walked in and could obviously see the confused look on my face.

"The toilet roll is for another game," she said. "For that game we have to wrap each other from head to toe and pretend we're mummies."

I turned to look at Mrs. Lurker because I was totally confused.

Lucy's mom didn't have any toilet paper wrapped around her, so I was sure I had missed something.

Maybe she puts it on after she uses the bathroom, I thought.

"If we have enough, we can even look like Ancient Egyptian Mummies," Lucy replied.

I just kept looking at Lucy's mom to see if I could make sense of what she was talking about, but I couldn't figure it out for the life of me.

"Bring some toilet tissue outside too," Lucy said.

That kind of made more sense to me, since back home we didn't have indoor toilets.

But Lucy took the rolls of toilet paper and set them up in the shape of a pyramid. It seemed that the final game we had to set up was called pumpkin bowling. The idea of that game was to roll pumpkins at the toilet paper pyramid to see if you can knock them over.

I guess the winner of the game gets to "go" first while everybody else has to wait their turn.

Now, while it was great fun helping Lucy prepare the Halloween party games, I was still really distracted. I couldn't get the image of those Zombies and Creepers out of my head. I needed time to formulate a plan to destroy them before they ate Lucy and all her family and friends.

I headed up stairs and sat down on Lucy's bed while she helped her mom put the finishing touches on all decorations.

How did the wizard boy manage to get the Minecraft mobs to come through the portal? I thought. *In fact, how did he create the portal in the first place? They don't have any obsidian here, do they?*

He must have some sort of special Minecraft power. But where did he get it? I closed my eyes and tried to remember what happened earlier. Was it his hat that gave him the power? Naw, it looked kind of homemade. Maybe it was his outfit? Nah...that looked kind of homemade too. But then, I remembered the magical staff!

Whoa! I remembered he held it over his head when he chanted the words. I bet the staff was the key to his power. I realized that I needed to find the wizard boy, steal his staff and return those Zombies and Creepers back to The Overworld before it was too late. But how to do it?

I figured my best bet was to head back to the wizard boy's house. If I found the boy, I'd find the staff.

Suddenly, my concentration was broken as I heard the sound of muffled music coming from downstairs. I opened the bedroom door and the music became louder.   I stood at the top of the stairs, preparing to go down, when the door bell rang. It seemed that the party was getting starting.

Lucy came running to answer the door in her witch outfit. Before she even pulled the door halfway open a group of little astronauts, princesses and pirates came flooding in. They all headed straight for the dining room table and began digging into the food. I started walking downstairs. This was my opportunity to sneak out the door and then secretly find my way back to the wizard boy's house. But, suddenly the doorbell rang again. I jumped back to the top of the stairs and looked down as Lucy answered the door again. To my horror, in through the door came the wizard boy!

He hugged Lucy. I couldn't see him really well, because Lucy was blocking my view. As he walked past her towards the living room I noticed he was carrying two things. In his left hand was a Halloween cake in a box. And in his right hand was the magical staff!

It was at that moment that I knew I had to do what I did best. I had to hide in a dark place and seize my chance to creep up to the wizard boy and take the staff. That was the only way I could save the town from a killer Minecraft mob attack!

Chapter 5
The Magic Staff

I reached the bottom of the stairs and glanced into the living room. Kids were dancing and eating the party food, and it seemed like they were having a fantastic time, completely oblivious to the terror that lurked only a few houses down the street.

I looked for the wizard boy, but couldn't see him. The room was pretty packed. He must have removed his hat or I would have seen it sticking out above everyone else. That made me think he knew I was onto him.

Just then, the lights went off. Mrs. Lurker turned the music up louder and some flashing disco lights came on. The party was in full swing, which created the perfect situation for me to find that staff. I sneaked into the living room, being sure to creep across the walls so I couldn't be seen. I realized my eyes were shining really bright so I tried to cover them up so that they wouldn't give me away.

Suddenly, a kid dressed as a Toilet Paper Mummy spotted me. He stared at my glowing eyes and took a step towards me to take a better look.

I realized I was right next to the disco lights. So, I put my hands in front of my eyes and moved them up and down. It made it look like my eyes were flashing, which blended into the disco lights perfectly. All of a sudden, the boy started to bounce up and down to the rhythm of the flashes coming from my eyes. Then the other kids started to join him. Next thing you know the whole room was dancing to the rhythm of my flashing eyes. So I was stuck there for at least four songs. Finally, they started some party games so the kids moved onto something else.

After, I moved around to where the wizard boy was. He was standing next to Lucy. More importantly, I couldn't believe how relaxed he looked considering he'd just released man-eating Zombies and exploding Creepers into the world.

But where was his staff?

I thought he would be holding it because it was so powerful, but I couldn't see it anywhere. He definitely had it with him when he entered the house, so I figured it had to be around there somewhere. I crept close to the wall and decided to move into the dining room to take a look.

Just then, Mrs. Lurker bumped into me. She was holding a plate of small cakes and asked me something. The music was so loud I couldn't hear a word she said. All I could see was the movement of her lips. I shook my square head and she moved on to the next kid.

I moved on quickly and eventually stepped into the dining room. This seemed to be the area where kids were keeping their stuff. So, if the staff was anywhere, surely it had to be there.

Then, as I moved people's stuff, I found what I was searching for. There, underneath a vampire cape was the wizard boy's magic staff! I grabbed it and felt a rush of energy flow through me. The power of the magical Minecraft staff was now mine. It was time to restore order to the human world, but first I had to get back in front of that Minecraft portal.

There was no way I was going to be able to sneak back though the house to the front door. There were way too many kids in the living room now, plus the doorbell had run again which meant more kids were flooding into the house. My only possible exit was through the back door. That meant moving through the kitchen where the lights were still on. I could see most of the kitchen from where I was standing. No one was in there, so I ran for it. I darted though the door, glanced over my shoulder and pulled on the handle of the back door.

The kitchen door swung open. I jumped though, closed it as quietly as I could behind me and dived behind the trashcan on the patio. I peered over the top as Mrs. Lurker walked into the kitchen, added some more food to her tray and then left again.

I breathed a huge sigh of relief. I had the magical staff. Now I had to find a way to get those Zombies and Creepers back to The Overworld and close that portal forever!

Chapter 6
Running from the Mob

I headed to the end of the back garden and stepped though the gate. On the other side was a poorly lit pathway but it seemed to run the full length of the street. It's times like these that make me really glad to have flashlights for eyeballs. So I followed the path to get to the wizard boy's house.

I began the journey to rediscover the Minecraft portal, but as I walked along I realized the short journey was going to be harder than I had imagined. I stumbled over soda cans, tripped over pizza boxes and a black cat darted out in front of me, scaring the living daylights out of me. Finally, I stepped in a huge wad of gum! My square foot was stuck to the concrete and I couldn't pull it free. Eventually, I managed to use the magic staff to lever my foot from the ground. Then it took me ten minutes to scrape the gum off my foot because of my thick, square fingers. And then it took another ten minutes to get the gum off of my fingers.

Eventually, I arrived at the back gate of the wizard boy's house. It was easy to find because of the giant Minecraft portal that stuck out in the back garden.

I crouched by the gate to allow my glowing eyes to light the area in front of me. I found the latch and lifted it. The gate creaked as I pushed it open, causing a dog to bark next door, but other than that no one seemed to notice.

I stepped into the garden and slowly approached the portal, holding the magic staff in front of me. I had no idea if any more mobs had been unleashed or whether any were about to jump out from the bushes.

I moved around to the front of the portal. A huge light shone onto the purple haze as it seemed to move in the light breeze. I looked around to make sure nobody else was near.

Once I was confident the coast was clear, I stood firm, planted the staff on the ground and began to chant. Except, I realized I didn't know what to say. So I just made it up as it came to me.

"Uh... Minecraft mobs away!...err... Minecraft mobs vanish!... Minecraft mobs go home already!"

But before I could complete my chants a floodlight on the back of the house turned on, filling the entire garden with light.

"Hey! Who's out there?" an angry man yelled.

I quickly turned around to see a hairy, bald man leaning out of an upstairs window in his white tank top. He squinted as he tried to focus. I stood as still as I could, hoping he wouldn't see me. But, he spotted me and started yelling inside at the lady in there with him.

"Hey! Marge! Call the cops, there's a weird looking square thing in our garden with a baseball bat."

It looked like I was in serious trouble! Suddenly, the hairy bald man came hurtling into the garden from the back door and lunged at me. I jumped to the side as he fell face down on the grass. He turned a weird shade of red and looked really sweaty. I think it was time for me to get out of there!

I ran down the side entrance and out into the street.

"There's a kid in a refrigerator box trying to rob us!" the man cried, running down his sidewalk as lights flicked on in every house in the street. "Grab him!"

Front doors flew open and people came running from their houses armed with wooden spoons, spatulas and any other potential weapon they could find. I turned towards Lucy's house and ran as fast as I could.

Still, I was no match for the pace of the mob! They formed together as a group and raced after me with their wooden spoons and spatulas waving angrily in the air. I don't know if it was the full moon or the fact that it was

Halloween, but it seemed like people were really angry for some reason. So I just ran as fast as I could.

I looked over my shoulder and the mob was gaining fast.

Just then, I spotted a house with large, rectangular pillars. It seemed I couldn't outrun the mob, so I needed a better plan. I darted up the steps to the house and hid behind one of the pillars. I held my breath and clutched the magical staff against my chest. Luckily, the mob continued shouting and ran straight past me. I waited for a minute for them to move further down the street, then I crept out and ran to Lucy's house, having one last look for the mob or any Zombies and Creepers on my way.

The moment I reached Lucy's house I bounded up the steps, opened the door, threw my body inside and slammed the door behind me, resting my back against it.

I'd had quite a fright. If the mob had caught me, I had no idea what would have happened. I was glad to be back in Lucy's house. At least I would be safe here.

It was then that I looked up. Every mini-monster in the room was staring at me. And the wizard boy was in front looking really, really mad.

Chapter 7
Into the Void

"**H**ey! The box kid stole my staff! Give it back!"

The wizard boy stepped forward and grabbed the staff, but I wasn't going to let go that easily. I tugged it towards my square body, but the wizard boy seemed to have powers greater than I had expected and yanked it back towards him. As I gave a final tug and pulled it back into my grasp, I glanced amongst the kids to search for Lucy. It was then that I saw the Zombies and Creepers! They were huddled at the back eating mini-sausages.

"ZOMBIES!" I cried. "CREEPERS! YOU'RE ALL IN DANGER! RUN FOR YOUR LIVES!"

I began pushing the kids towards the door as they shouted at me and tried to push me back. I couldn't believe they weren't as terrified as I was. I realized I needed to take drastic action. If the kids weren't going to run for safety I had to find a way of destroying the Minecraft mobs there and then.

As I ran though a few ideas in my head, the wizard boy seized his chance. He lunged towards me once more, this time catching me off guard and stealing the magic staff back.

I pushed past him hoping he wouldn't turn me into a Slime or Spider and dashed into the garden. I ran to Mr. Lurker's shed, unbolted the door and leapt inside. Cobwebs wrapped around me as I searched for a shovel. I found a pair of gardening gloves, a screwdriver and a few dead mice, but no shovel. Then, I spotted it. I grabbed the handle of the shovel and pulled it from the mess.

I ran back into the garden as all the kids and
Mrs. Lurker moved onto the patio to watch
what I was doing.

I looked down at the soil, gripped the shovel
tightly and plunged it into the ground and
started digging. I pushed it in again and again.

Suddenly, Lucy appeared at my side with the
usual confused look on her face.

"What are you doing?" she whispered. "Have you lost it? Plus, since you're my friend, you're making me look crazy too!"

"There's no other way to get rid of them!" I replied as the hole in front of me got deeper by the second.

"Getting rid of who?" Lucy questioned.

"The Minecraft Mobs!"

"What Minecraft mobs? Herobrine, I think you're going crazy. I think the full moon has done something to you."

"Think what you want," I protested. "But look over there. That's a Creeper and that one over there is a Zombie. I need to save all of your lives!"

"Herobrine!" Lucy shouted. "That's Doug!"

"It's not dug yet, but I'm getting there," I replied.

I jumped down into the hole that was now almost as deep as me. I had to keep digging. I had to dig as deep as I could until I reached The Void. Lucy might have thought I was nuts, but my plan was going working, that was until Mr. Lurker arrived home.

He stepped into the empty house and headed straight for the patio where everyone was.

"HEY! KID! WHAT ARE YOU DOING TO MY LAWN?!!"

His voice scared me more than those Creepers did! I dropped the shovel into the hole and turned around. Mr. Lurker's face was redder than a baboon's bottom and he looked like a bull about to charge. I quickly jumped out of the hole. With everyone staring at me with angry looks, and steam beginning to flood out of Mr. Lurker's nostrils, I realized I needed to start running... *again!*

Chapter 8
The Chase

I realized I couldn't save everybody, but I was determined to save Lucy. I grabbed her by the wrist and ran though the sea of people into the house as Mr. Lurker stretched out his huge hands, trying to grab me. Lucy kept yelling my name but I didn't have time to listen. We ran up the stairs, into Lucy's bedroom and I threw the door shut as quickly as I could.

I looked around. There was work to be done.

I leaned against her dresser and pushed it across the door. I pulled the bed towards the door too, and just in time. Suddenly, there was knocking and banging on the other side of the door.

"It's the Creepers and Zombies!" I cried. "They're trying to get in!"

They started thumping against the door with all their weight. The dresser drawer began to move.

"We need to get out of here!" I yelled.

I looked over at the window and then at Lucy.
I slid the window up and saw that directly
outside was a huge oak tree. A branch as thick
as my body stretched out right in front of the
window. With Minecraft mobs at the door, it
was our only chance of escaping.

"Follow me!" I yelled as I made my way onto
the branch.

"You're crazy!" Lucy shouted.

But, before she could think about the situation
any more, her dad screamed from the other
side of the door.

"Lucy! I blame you for this. You brought that
weird square kid into our house. When I get in
there, you're grounded for a month!"

That was enough to scare Lucy into action.
She climbed onto the branch behind me and
we made our way quickly and carefully to the
bottom.

Lucy's bedroom was at the front of the house, so the moment our feet touched the sidewalk, we ran. One of the kids in Lucy's house was standing at the bottom of the stairs and saw us make our escape. She yelled and alerted everyone else, and within seconds we had everyone chasing after us.

And the mob that was chasing us was big! There was Mr. and Mrs. Lurker, the wizard boy with his magic staff and a whole host of mini-monsters including werewolves, ghouls, pirates, astronauts, several man-eating Zombies and a few exploding Creepers. Yikes!

We ran to the end of the street. I paused wondering which way to go. Suddenly, the mob that had been chasing us rounded the corner of the street.

"There he is!" cried the hairy bald man. "It's the box boy with the glowing eyes. Get him!"

The charge of the other mob only left us with one direction to turn. That was towards the

Recreation Hall at the top of the hill. I ran towards the Rec Hall gates as quickly as I could and Lucy did the same. Getting caught by her dad was not the way she wanted this Halloween night to end.

As we entered the Rec Hall I looked around. There was a huge field with white lines marked on it and a concrete basketball court in the far corner. To the left was a small hut that appeared to be a café. Obviously, at this time of night it was closed.

To the side of the café was a play area with several climbing frames and a long zip line wire that ran from a large wooden play fort to the ground. The fort seemed like the best place to hide, so we sprinted across the field towards it.

The field was poorly lit, so as the mobs arrived at the Rec Hall gate they lost sight of us for a moment.

As I panted I could hear them discussing where we could be. Then, the wizard boy saw

us. I don't know how as it was pretty dark. I assumed he must have used his magic staff to conjure up a location spell or something. Either way, the chase was on once more.
We headed past the café and into the play fort. Some ladders ran up to a second floor inside the fort. I climbed to the top with Lucy behind me and we peered out through the battlements.

"What do we do now?" Lucy asked.

I didn't answer. To be honest, I had no idea. I knew I needed to get back to the wizard boy's garden, but without the magic staff it seemed the only option I had to prevent the spread of Minecraft mobs was to destroy the portal completely. But, that meant that the Creepers and Zombies that were already in the real world would be stuck here. That seemed fine if it was limited to only those four mobs, but if they spawned then who knows what could happen.

Suddenly, a flashlight beam hit my face. It seemed my glowing eyes had given away our location!

"There he is!" cried Mr. Lurker. "There's the glowing eyed kid who's kidnapped my daughter!"

Chapter 9
The Rec Hall

The mob thundered towards us as the flood-lights burst on across the Rec Hall.

The kids were quicker than the adults, so the first wave of attacks came from the pirates, astronauts and goblins. They moved to the bottom of the ladder. We were running out of places to go.

Lucy and I ran along the fort, but as they climbed to the top of the ladder we realized we were trapped. The wizard boy took the lead and brandished his magic staff in front of him.

"He's going to do magic!" I cried. "Stand behind me, Lucy! I'll protect you. I won't let him turn you into a Slime!"

"Herobrine," Lucy replied. "He won't turn me into..."

Before she could finish her sentence, I spotted something that would give us the perfect exit.

I grabbed Lucy's arm and pulled her with me. I was heading towards the zip line. I climbed on and Lucy grabbed a hold of me. I had no idea if it would take the weight of us both together, but it was our only chance. I closed my eyes, held on tight and lifted my feet.

As the wizard boy swung his magic staff at me, Lucy and I shot from the play fort, narrowly avoiding his spell. The moment we hit the ground we ran for the café as the mob of monster kids descended the ladder and headed in our direction once more.

"The door's shut!" Lucy shouted, trying to turn the handle. "There's no way of getting in."

That didn't worry me. I took ten steps back and then I ran toward the door. I threw my square head against the door and tumbled into the dark café, crashing onto the black and white tiles. Lucy followed.

We searched around for somewhere to hide. The mob knew we were in there so crawling under a table didn't seem like an option. Then, with no time left to find the perfect hiding place we simply hid behind the counter. Lucy covered my glowing eyes so that the mob couldn't tell where we were.

The mini werewolves and pirates entered the café behind us, followed by Mr. and Mrs. Lurker. I could hear Mr. Lurker's heavily booted feet plodding around. Tables and chairs screeched on the tiled floor as he searched every inch of the café looking for us.

Then, I heard him walking towards us. It appeared there was nowhere left for him to search except behind the counter. I decided there and then that I wasn't going to just crouch there and be captured, so I knew it was time to fight back!

There was a huge tray of cream pies beside us. I picked one up, held it in my trembling hand and waited for Mr. Lurker to lean over the countertop. The second he did, I pushed the pie into his mad-looking face and it squished into him like a square boot into a poop patch. But, something began to happen to him. His face turned a really bright red and got so hot that the cream pie melted away and dripped onto the floor.

I think I was in some serious trouble.

Chapter 10
Battle at the Café

Mr. Lurker stood up straight. I grabbed another cream pie. I don't know what possessed me to do it. Looking back now, I would have been better off just coming out from behind the counter and surrendering. But that's not what I did. I took the pie, aimed it at the wizard boy and let it fly!

The wizard boy stumbled back in shock, then he turned to the table behind him that had a plate of moldy sandwiches on it. Next thing I know they were flying through the air headed my way.

I ducked behind the counter as the sandwich cannon balls smashed against the wall above me. I grabbed some more cream pies and waited for the last of the sandwiches to shoot over my head. Then, I unleashed the fury!

Like some sort of crazy food cannon, I pelted one child after another with cream pies. Most hit their target and sent the kids running from the café crying for their moms. It was total carnage.

Chocolate chip cookies shot across the café like mini Frisbees, fairy cakes catapulted around the room as if a medieval battle was going on, and long jelly rolls fired like torpedoes with built-in homing devices.

I have to admit, my aim was pretty good. But, one particular cream pie went astray. I'd never do anything to harm Mrs. Lurker. After all, she'd been so good to me over the past few weeks. But this was a situation that had quickly gotten out of control. I threw a pie, aiming for a tall kid dressed like a pony, but he dived out of the way and the cream pie hit Mrs. Lurker right in the face.

It seemed the attack on his wife was a step too far! Mr. Lurker had had enough. He leaned over the counter, grabbed my square head and pulled me into the air.

"I've got him! " he yelled, as all the kids and the mob outside let out a colossal cheer!

I know it was Halloween, but this witch-hunt had gotten out of control!

He dragged me back onto the sports field and began to cart me towards the street. I didn't know if we were heading to the police station or the Lurker's house. Seeing the look Mr. Lurker's face, I quietly hoped we were heading to see the cops. I had a feeling they'd be more forgiving. But, as we passed the police station it was clear that the destination was Lucy's house. I realized at that moment, I had to escape.

I couldn't understand it. After all, all I wanted to do was save them all from the man-eating Zombies and exploding Creepers. No one seemed to appreciate everything I was trying to do. Then I thought about what the Zombies and Creepers would do to Lucy if I was caught. As I started thinking about it, I started getting madder and madder. Then I felt my eyes glowing red hot. I looked at Mr. Lurker's arm. Suddenly, a blast shot out of my eyes and hit Mr. Lurker right on the elbow. He let go of me with a squeal. And as I dropped to the floor, I took my chance. I could see the wizard boy's house. I ran towards it as fast as I could. The Minecraft portal had to be destroyed!

Chapter 11
Face-off at the Portal

I busted through the side gate of the wizard boy's house and could hear the crowd in pursuit. I ran through into the garden, and there it was – the Minecraft Portal!

I quickly searched for something to destroy it with. There was nothing around except a rake and a water hose. I'd never tried to destroy a portal before, but I figured neither of those would get the job done.

Suddenly, I heard the side gate swing open. I had to hide. The backdoor to the house was open, so I dashed inside, switched off all the lights and hid behind the couch.

I kept as still as I could, and covered my
glowing eyes as I heard the mob stampede into
the back garden.

"Where is he?" I heard Mr. Lurker cry.

"He's not behind the portal," a boy replied.

"Check the shed," another added.

I could hear them turning things upside down as they looked everywhere for me.

I could see the front door. Part of me wanted to quietly make my escape – to leave the town and never return. But, if I did that the portal would stay open and more Minecraft monsters will enter through the portal and take over the human world. And what about Lucy? After thinking about it for a few seconds, I realized that wasn't an option.

I peered over the top of the couch. I could see through the French doors at the back of the room into the garden. Someone glanced my way. I gasped and lowered my head quickly.

I held still. It was then that I felt a warm breath beside my ear. I slowly turned my head. I was staring face to face with the wizard boy's dog!

I tried to smile but I could tell the dog was really mad that I was in its house. I was a stranger all right, and I guess I was a weird looking one at that!

I held still as long as I could – then the dog attacked!

It lunged at me, gnashing its teeth. I had no option. I leapt over the top of the couch and ran into the back garden with the big, hairy dog chasing after me.

I ran into the garden, tripping over a small step and crawling through the legs of the mob. After I got through the crowd, I found myself right in front of the portal. The mob went silent. I stood up. Lucy was at the front. I grabbed her hand and pulled her forward.

"Let her go!" cried the wizard boy, holding out his staff.

"Don't you try and use that magic staff on me," I cried. "Or I'll jump into the portal!"

The wizard boy held his staff higher and stepped forwards. As he did, I could see the Creepers and Zombies advancing behind him. I had tried my best to escape, but I could see I had no options left. I grabbed Lucy tight, closed my eyes and jumped into the portal!

I expected to feel something weird as I headed into another dimension. I hadn't been through a Minecraft portal in a long time, but I do remember that the experience was really trippy. But I was really worried about Lucy. I didn't know what effect going into the Minecraft world was going to have on her.

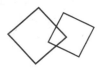

After a few seconds, for some strange reason I didn't feel anything. So, I took a deep breath and opened my eyes. To my complete surprise, I was still standing in the wizard boy's garden. I was facing the shed and the back gate with the portal behind me.

Suddenly, Lucy pulled away from me and climbed back though the portal.

I couldn't believe it. What was she doing? I kind of had a feeling that jumping though the portal several times would probably be bad for her health.

But then I took a look at the outer structure of the portal. It seemed more flimsy than any portal I remembered from The Overworld. Still, we were in the human world now, so maybe this was how Minecraft portals were supposed to look here.

I tapped on it. It sounded hollow. Then, I examined the purple glow in the middle. I stuck my hand in it, expecting it to react. But, nothing happened. I grabbed a stick from the garden and shoved it through the middle. To my surprise, it seemed to just pass through some sort of purple fabric.

Then I decided to look through the center. I poked my head through as the purple curtain parted. Unfortunately, on the other side, the mob was still there waiting for me. Except Lucy was also there, and this time, with Zombies and Creepers standing next to her!

Chapter 12
The Spooky Truth

I was in shock. The purple haze was just an old purple curtain, and the Minecraft portal was flimsy. It looked like the Minecraft portal was a fake!

But, then how did the Zombies and Creepers get into the real world? I thought.

As one of the Creepers held Lucy's arm, I felt my body stiffen up. I was scared for Lucy. I didn't want to make any sudden movements in case the Creeper was about to explode. I was going to have to remain calm.

"Take it easy and walk slowly towards me," I whispered to Lucy as the mob stared at me, each of them with a frown on their face.

"What?" Lucy replied.

"A Creeper is holding your arm," I added. "Just remain calm, and slowly slide my way and he just might not explode."

"What are you talking about, Herobrine?"

"I'm going to dig another hole so that we can get out of here."

"But, it's Doug!"

"The hole's not dug yet, but give me a minute."

"No!" Lucy said, raising her voice in frustration. "This is Doug. He just dressed up as a Creeper for Halloween. And these are his friends. They're all dressed up like Creepers and Zombies for Halloween too."

The four of them pulled off their masks and underneath were four regular kids with very confused looks upon their faces.

"You mean, they were just dressed up this whole time?"

"Yes! That's what people do on Halloween. They dress up," Lucy said.

Then all of the other mini-monsters took off their masks to reveal a bunch of young kids who looked really, really mad.

"Haven't you learned anything this evening?"

To be honest, I was more confused than ever!

"What about the wizard boy and his magic staff?" I asked.

"The wizard boy?" Lucy questioned. "Oh! That's Ned. He always dresses as a wizard on Halloween."

"The staff is only a plastic stick my mom bought from the toy store," Ned said. "Is that why you stole it? You thought it had magic powers?"

"Well... Then how else did you get the Creepers and Zombies though the portal?"

"The whole portal thing was just a fun Halloween idea we had," Ned said. "We thought it would be fun to dress up as mobs and make a portal out of cardboard boxes and an old curtain."

All of a sudden some of the kids in the crowd started to giggle. And then more people started to chuckle. Next thing I know the whole crowd was on the ground roaring in laughter. Even Lucy was holding her sides and cackling like a witch.

Well, I didn't know what else to say. Half the town was in the wizard boy's garden laughing their heads off.

After a long while of non-stop laughing, the crowd soon dispersed, chuckling on the way. The wizard boy and his parents headed back into their house, leaving just me, Lucy and her parents in the garden.

"You know, Herobrine," Mr. Lurker said, trying to catch his breath from laughing. "You caused some real trouble this evening. You've had the whole town chasing you around and heaven knows what the owners of that café at the Rec

Hall will say when they walk in tomorrow. Come on, let's head home."

So, Mr. and Mrs. Lurker headed down the sideway into the street and Lucy and I followed behind them.

Lucy's house wasn't too far away, yet the walk seemed to take forever. All I noticed were kids staring out of their windows, pointing at me and laughing.

I had been chased for most of the night and I kind of felt like I needed some time alone before heading back to Lucy's house.

"I'm just going to go for a walk," I said to Lucy. "It's been a long night."

Lucy agreed that was probably a good idea.

"Don't be too long, though," she said. "Mom will probably be getting some hot chocolate ready, so don't let it get cold."

"I won't," I replied.

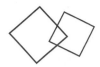

Lucy and her mom and dad headed on down the street, chuckling and giggling as they walked up the steps to her house. I stood beneath the street lamp wondering where I could go where the neighbors wouldn't be laughing at me and pointing fingers. I spotted a small, quiet street leading off from the main road. I wandered towards it, looked around and then began to take a slow walk down the street.

In the sky the moon was still as full and bright as ever. I heard an owl hoot and in the distance and what sounded like a wolf howling.

I took a deep breath. I didn't know if it was the spooky atmosphere or the full moon, but something weird had definitely gotten into me that night.

How could I have been so stupid? I thought.

As I continued down the street I noticed a subtle mist beginning to fill the air. I was just about to turn back when a house further ahead caught my eye. It was a huge house with a tower on the side, two giant electrodes sticking out of the roof and a weathervane on the top that spun almost uncontrollably. I stopped in front of it. There was a black wrought iron gate leading to some well worn steps and a black wooden door. I opened the gate slowly. I felt compelled to go in.

The gate creaked as if it hadn't been moved in over a hundred years. Tumbleweeds sat on the sides of the stone steps leading up to the front door and a small skeleton of a dead rodent lay in the overgrown garden.

As I reached the door I lifted my hand to knock, but suddenly I felt scared. I decided to take a further look around first. I crept along the old porch towards one of the tall windows and slowly peered in.

Inside I could see a huge room that looked like a library. And inside the library there was a giant computer screen, with what appeared to be a scene from Minecraft on it. There were two huge wires coming out of the computer monitor and running across the room. I moved to the other side of the window to get a better look. To my surprise, on the opposite side of the room was a giant Minecraft portal. It was made of black obsidian and glowed with its usual purple haze. I rubbed my eyes and looked again.

What? Another Minecraft Portal?!! I thought as the hairs on the back of my square head began to stand up.

Then, I shook my head and laughed. There was no way I was going to fall for that again!

I walked briskly back along the porch, down the steps and out through the creaky gate. I looked back at the house as the purple glow from the room got brighter.

As I closed the gate I noticed the name of the house carved into a stone sign beside the gate. The place was called *"Herobrine's Mansion."*

Whoa. I never knew there were other people in the human world named Herobrine...That is so cool.

So, as I walked away and caught sight of the purple glowing portal in the living room once more I smiled. Halloween night had certainly been a treat, but there was no way I was going to be tricked in that way again!

The End

and

Happy Halloween!

Leave Us a Review

Please support us by leaving a review. The more reviews we get the more books we will write!

And if you really liked this book, please tell a friend. I'm sure they will be happy you told them about it.

Check Out Our Other Books from Zack Zombie Publishing

The Diary of a Minecraft Zombie
Book Series

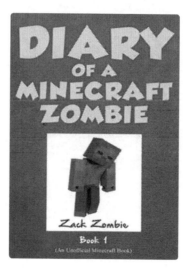

Get The Entire Series on
Amazon Today!

The Ultimate Minecraft Comic Book Series

Get The Entire Series on
Amazon Today!

Herobrine's Wacky Adventures

Get The Entire Series on
Amazon Today!

The Mobbit
An Unexpected Minecraft Journey

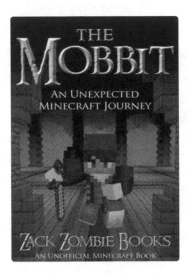

Get The Entire Series on Amazon Today!

Steve Potter and the Endermen's Stone

Get The Entire Series on
Amazon Today!

An Interview With a Minecraft Mob

Get The Entire Series on Amazon Today!

Minecraft
Galaxy Wars

Get The Entire Series on
Amazon Today!

Ultimate Minecraft Secrets:
An Unofficial Guide to Minecraft Tips, Tricks and Hints to Help You Master Minecraft

Get Your Copy on
Amazon Today!

42299648R00057

Made in the USA
San Bernardino, CA
30 November 2016